# Uniquely Yours

## A Collection of Over 700 Suggestions to Individualize Your Wedding

by

### Michelle M. Pattarozzi

*Illustrations by Julikay Barr*

*To Ed...*
*For his unending support and encouragement.*

*Published by Just Imagine, 105 Iron Bark Ct., East Peoria, IL 61611*

## ACKNOWLEDGMENTS

**Special thanks to Mrs. Florence Blocki and Mrs. Julikay Barr for their research and contributions to this book.**

*Dear Bride-To-Be:*

*Many exciting and delightful "details" await your attention! Details to be tended to throughout the upcoming months that will insure a perfect wedding and inspire a memorable occasion. The primary purpose of this booklet is to help you individualize the specific details of your "total plan". "Uniquely Yours" is a collection of over 700 suggestions to assist you in attaining a warm, one-of-a-kind, distinctly personal day.*

*Planning your wedding takes organizational skill and there's work involved too, but it can and should be fun — perhaps even moreso when family and friends are involved. Rise above the ordinary in a joyous shared experience. Incorporate your own personalities and personal feelings into your plans, but remember to take into consideration the feelings of others who are involved and those closest to you.*

*As you read through the following pages, use your imagination and allow your mind to expand on the ideas I have expressed. For example, ideas suggested for showers and pre-nuptial parties might prove interesting for small receptions or rehearsal parties. Ideas suggested for bridal bouquets and attendants' bouquets might be reversed. Etc....*

*Be creative! Don't be afraid to suggest "something different" to your baker, caterer, florist... anyone who may be helping you.*

*And in the way of some personal advice...*

**Share your ideas...**

    **Follow your heart's desire...**

        **and Laugh at the unexpected.**

*May your lives be as filled with happiness and laughter as your hearts are filled with love.*

*Michelle M. Pattarozzi*

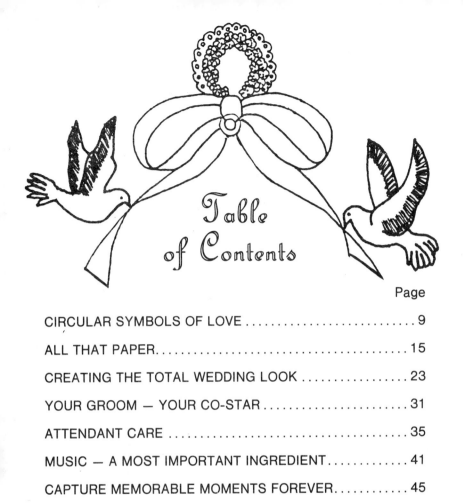

# Table of Contents

Best Wishes
On
Your Wedding

Circular
Symbols of Love

# CIRCULAR SYMBOLS OF LOVE

A ring on the third finger of the left hand definitely says something to people. It might proclaim "She will be getting married soon." or "He's already married." To the giver and the wearer, however, these rings carry a far deeper meaning. They serve as visual reminders of promises to love and to be faithful. *Your* rings may be as personal and unique as this love shared by the two of you.

As a symbol of engagement, the diamond has endured — a tradition that dates back to Early Italy where there was a superstition that the diamond was born of the flames of love. A classic solitaire paired with a simple band is always beautiful, but *not* the only option and, though the most popular diamond cut is the tiffany (round), if you opt for high style in a diamond engagement ring, consider an alternative cut such as the oval, pear, marquise, heart or emerald-shaped stone. Jewelry designers continually update traditional styles to blend with contemporary tastes. Geometric and delicate free-form mountings are available featuring two-tone white and yellow gold combinations, accenting smaller diamonds and channel setting — a stone-on-stone design.

To focus on the uncommon, consider a free-form, perhaps a small heart of gold, or another gem circled by diamonds, or a sapphire set off by diamond baguettes or a setting of stones alternating diamonds with color — emerald, aquamarine, peridot, amethyst, garnet, etc... Your personal setting might include a diamond, your birthstone, his birthstone and/or any combination of precious gems you desire. Consider criss-crossing bands to enhance your jewels.

Wedding bands traditionally are gleaming bands of gold, white gold or platinum, sometimes encrusted with jewels. A band with intertwining rows of diamonds might serve as a combination engagement and wedding ring. A bit out of the ordinary, but also available, are bands of pink gold (appears very similar to copper) and green gold.

Check with your jeweler for matched his n' hers sets. You might choose with the idea of adding an "anniversary touch" — a band designed so that you can insert additional stones in years to come — perhaps one every five years.

Consider custom-designed rings. Capture everyone's eye with a stunning contemporary design, perhaps wide bands of highly polished gold and square in shape. Yours might don a regally perched ruby on a glimmering, smooth surface. There's more to a square shape than its elegant design. Stones will always show because the ring is not as likely to turn as a round ring and fingers are not pressured because the sides of the ring are flat.

In addition to her engagement and wedding rings, a bride might choose to wear a guard ring as well, particularly where it provides the double function of protecting the stone-bearing engagement ring and acting as an interface between it and the wedding band. When placed on the finger the guard ring sometimes forms a Chinese lock combining all three bands into a single unit.

What if you find the perfect ring at a not-so-perfect price? A professional jeweler can change the setting, stone, size, cut — even the amount of gold — without losing the particular look you desire.

A personal added touch to a possession you will always cherish is an inscription inside your wedding band or bands if it is a double ring ceremony. In lieu of the traditional initials and date have your jeweler engrave the first letters of an individualized statement reflective of your love and commitment! — ie

*"Our Love Is A Gift We'll Treasure Forever"*
                                        Code    *"OLIAGWTF"*
*"May Our Love Enrich Our Being"Code      "MOLEOB"*

You might choose a favorite line of poetry or compose a short message with half being engraved in your wedding band and the other half in your groom's band.

For assistance in composing your own message, information regarding engraving and more ideas for unique ring designs, consult a reputable jeweler.

## An Added Gesture During the Ceremony

Most couples in the United States today seem to prefer the double-ring ceremony. Marriage is a giving-receiving relationship and the use of a ring for the groom as well as the bride perhaps more clearly symbolizes this belief. Both give, both receive a circular sign of commitment.

An added personal gesture by the man and woman during the exchange of wedding bands can further stress this concept of giving-receiving. By placing the ring only part way on her finger as he pronounces the vows, the groom indicates his giving of himself to her. As she draws it on the rest of the way, the bride shows her acceptance of that gift, of that commitment. Naturally, this slight, but significant addition can be employed in either the single or double-ring service.

# — Notes to Myself —

As We Start Our Life Together...

Mr. & Mrs.

Thank you friends and neighbors
and relatives so dear
for all the joys you've wished us
and for your presence here

Now when this day is over
and our guests have gone away
the memory of this joyous time
will ever with us stay

Sally and Dan
June 1, 1983

Sally + Dan
June 1, 1983

All That Paper

# ALL THAT PAPER

## Invitations

Wedding invitations carry a distinct message, and like the many aspects of your total plan, you have options about the way this "special message" is sent. Traditionally, invitations are inserted into an envelope which is then inserted into a mailing envelope. They use extremely formal language following all of the rules of the Queen's English and an engraved typeface that looks like old-world lettering.

Although etiquette books may suggest engraved invitations, there is no need to undertake the additional expense unless you feel strongly that it's really what you want. Engraved invitations are made on metal plates, and, should you choose them, you may ask your stationer to give you this plate. Many creative brides have put these plates to good decorative use.

Printed invitations can be just as lovely and there are many styles available at much more reasonable prices. Ask to see the printer's selection of typefaces. Consider Roman type for a very dignified look; Script for a look of romance. Invitations are traditionally sent out by the parents of the bride, though the names of the groom's parents have been turning up more and more in acknowledgment of their importance and the fact that they are often involved in sharing the ever-increasing wedding expenses. The couple may issue invitations themselves if they are giving the wedding.

Before choosing a particular invitation, view a wide selection of the many, many available styles. You might choose a simple, old-fashioned design or one of the many available contemporaries. Your invitation might don a photograph of you and your groom — perhaps an engagement picture. This idea is especially nice if relatives of either the bride or the groom are not familiar with the other. You might choose a quotation with special meaning or a particular Bible verse to be included; perhaps a style that has meaning to you or one that makes a modern or personal statement.

Nearly transparent parchment, shiny metallic papers, colored papers, colored inks and colored borders are also available. There are invitations with deckle-edging, floral panels, foil-lined envelopes (copper, gold, silver), colored envelope flaps, hot-stamped foil and unique folds. The artistic bride may even choose to design her own invitation with personal wording.

If it's a small wedding you are planning, you may decide to phone or handwrite personal invitations. The smaller the guest list, the easier it may be to think of clever, creative ways to extend an invitation. For example, in a small community, you might have each invitation tied to a balloon and personally delivered by a friend dressed in a tuxedo. How about hand-delivered scrolls? Add a tiny silk flower or perhaps a holly sprig with berries (during the holiday season) to each invitation. Use your imagination!

Play up holiday themes in your invitations. Use red or green ink on a wintry white background for December, pink or red in February, etc... Arrange to have the paper or envelopes scented — bayberry, cinnamon, strawberry, lavender, etc... Or, for a really unique touch, include an enclosure — tiny gold and silver paper stars, rose petals or candy hearts that will spill out when the invitation is opened.

Where invitations traditionally read "requesting the pleasure of your company", leave a blank space and personalize each invitation by writing in the name of each invited guest in black ink. Just ask your printer to rearrange the lines so you will have enough space.

A single card might serve as a less formal alternative to the conventional two-panel folded invitation, perhaps with printing over a background design or photo. Another unusual option — have your invitation message printed on wide, colored satin ribbon.

Emphasize the fact that your friends and relatives are

invited to sit in a special area by sending either pew cards or "within-the-ribbons" cards to indicate a seat within a reserved section.

Have the street address of the church printed on the invitation. It isn't customary, but it's practical, especially if you're being married in a large city where there are likely to be several churches with similar names.

Consider sending directions with the invitations. They can be printed on small enclosure cards. This isn't traditional either, but again, it *can* be practical. You might have them printed to match the look of the invitation. Another solution is to mail out maps separately, perhaps after R.S.V.P.'s are received.

Ask your printer to have outside envelopes delivered earlier so you will have more time for addressing.

## The Wedding Announcement

The wedding announcement — it looks like a wedding invitation, but it is sent after the ceremony. It lets people know when, where and to whom you were married. There is no need to send announcements to anyone receiving an invitation.

This time-honored way of telling friends your news is making a comeback. Ask your printer to show you paper stock and lettering styles. If you consider the traditional style — engraved lettering on ecru or ivory stock — a bit too formal, you can send a personal note or telephone each person who won't be at the wedding. You might wish to include a note that you'll be visiting for the holidays, an invitation to a second reception in another part of the country or a snapshot of the two of you.

## At-Home Cards

If you have a new address, printed at-home cards are a nice way to help your friends keep track of you. These might be included with announcements or thank you notes or sent out separately. Include your names, address and zip code, phone number and perhaps a special message. A bride who chooses to retain her maiden name (or hyphenate it) should do so on the at-home cards.

## Thank Yous

Soon after your invitations have been mailed out, wedding gifts will begin arriving. The wise bride-to-be will record all gifts in a wedding notebook and will do her very best to keep her thank you notes up-to-date. To acknowledge gifts received before the wedding, you might want to use stationery carrying your maiden name.

When you are having your wedding invitations printed, ask the printer to show you a selection of "informals". An informal is note-size paper folded in half (like a card) with your name(s) (or initials) printed on the top sheet. After your thank yous are written, you may use them later for personal notes, informal invitations or gift-enclosure cards.

Be creative when saying "Thank You". You might tuck a snapshot in with each note that shows you using the gift. Write your thank you messages on valentines or consider having thank you postcards printed with a wedding picture and space for a personal message.

When sending thank yous, don't forget all those little favors people may have done for you. Mail notes to friends — maybe a neighbor accepted delivered gifts when you weren't home, or your co-workers arranged accommodations for out-of-town guests, or your hairdresser opened especially early on your wedding day to style hair for the entire bridal party. With your thank you message, include a mention of the gesture and how it helped.

## The Printed Program

Perhaps you and your fiance are writing your own ceremony or perhaps your ceremony includes customs that may be unfamiliar to your guests. Perhaps you'll want everyone in the church to join in a responsive reading. Whatever your ceremony includes, guests will be able to follow along if you provide a printed program.

Consider the following suggestions, then decide what to include in accordance to your format and personal preference: Your name and that of your groom — as they appear on formal invitations or simply your first names; date, time and place of the ceremony, names of clergy, the order of the service, members of the wedding party, organist, other musicians, soloist, choir members, your musical selections — perhaps a special reason why you chose them, names of your parents and other close relatives (younger brothers and sisters, grandparents) who are not a part of your wedding party, any person in a special role, site of the reception that follows (perhaps with directions or a map), a personal note of welcome from both of you or of thanks to your families and/or your guests, perhaps a special message or poem, a bit about how the two of you first met or your first date, your new address and phone number.

Have your ushers place programs in each pew prior to the arrival of guests or designate a special "wedding helper" to hand them out from a decorated basket as guests arrive. You might opt for a one-page program printed on a duplicating machine, a professionally printed booklet with a cover designed by you and your groom or anything in between.

In lieu of an entire printed program, you may wish to distribute copies of a welcome message, prayer, poem or special message only. In any case, do check to see what stationery stores, printers and religious supply sources have to offer that you might be able to work into your plans.

**Scrolls**

Personalized parchment scrolls make a charming addition to the wedding, and can be given out as the guests leave the ceremony or as favors at the reception. Unrolled, they may be used as or enclosed with thank you notes. Wedding scrolls are available through many wedding stationers and bridal accessory shops. They may be printed with a thank you message, a biblical verse, a poem, your "recipe for a happy marriage" or whatever message you wish and are personalized with the names of you and your groom and your wedding date.

The scrolls may be rolled up and tied with colored ribbon or secured with gold or silver decorating rings or any other novelty wedding accessory you might desire.

## Other Accessories

You may choose to shop for a "creative" napkin style — beverage napkins or luncheon size. There are many available with "cute" pictures, romantic quotations, foil monograms, elegant borders, etc... If you want something different, consider colored napkins with a center design and colored ink to reflect your total wedding color scheme. Do order several hundred extra napkins for use on anniversaries and special occasions during the years to come. Check into matchbook designs and Father- and Mother-Of-The-Bride cards — available at many bridal accessory shops. These cards add an extra element of fun for Mom and/or Dad on that special day.

## Calligraphy

Calligraphy, the art of decorative lettering, will add a formal, polished note to your wedding accessories. It makes *everything* in print look beautiful and creative. Have your invitation written by a calligrapher and then printed from the calligrapher's copy. The same would apply to announcements, response cards, reception cards, informals, programs, etc... Consider a calligraphed "Welcome Message" to stand on an easel at the reception entrance, calligraphed reception wall banners, seating chart, placecards, table #'s, coasters, cake bags, etc...

Creating the
Total Wedding Look

# CREATING THE
# TOTAL WEDDING LOOK

## Your Bridal Outfit

As a small child in the "days of make believe", you might have stood in front of a mirror with a curtain pinned to the top of your head wearing mom's lipstick and favorite high heels dreaming of the day you would walk down the aisle in a bouffant gown with oodles of ruffles, billowy sleeves and full, flowing skirt with lengthy train. You pictured it all. You imagined just the way you wanted it to be. Your tastes may have changed or you may still feel exactly the same. Whatever your personal style preference, begin your search for that "special look" by browsing through copies of current bridal magazines such as *Bride's* and *Modern Bride*. These magazines offer pages and pages of bridal fashions, attendants' gowns and helpful information. Clip and save photos of appealing gowns and organize them in a small notebook.

Write down what it is about a particular gown that you like. Is it the tiers of lace, off the shoulder ruffles, wispy net sleeves, pleats, the scalloped hem or the bodice festooned with pearls? Take your notebook when you go shopping. Instead of trying to describe the "dress of your dreams", you will be able to show pictures that explain it.

Fashion trends and practicality have contributed to the creation of bridal looks such as that of wedding separates — a lacy, long skirt paired perhaps, with a sleeveless blouson or scooped-neck top. Slim, tailored designs and mid-calf flowing, handkerchief hemlines are available. One-piece dresses that look like blouses and skirts are casual and easy to move in. A billowy, tea-length skirt with petal hem may provide that romantic look for a garden wedding or lacy, spirited pantaloons accented with a traditional floral veil may mark your personal distinction. You may consider a sophisticated, just-below-the-knee-length suit or, if your budget is limited, an appealing bridesmaid's dress in white or ivory.

Planning to marry outdoors? Pure white and lacy will

look prettiest, but a pastel underskirt may lend a country air. If you are planning to marry in the fall or winter, consider an elegant pure white shawl — angora, long cashmere or hand-crocheted. A velvet jacket with ruffles or a fur capelet will feel luxurious over your lacy wedding dress. A puff-sleeved bolero would look lovely over an empire-waisted gown.

More and more, bridal dresses are being featured with "just a touch" of color. Embroider a tiny blue flower at the bottom of your skirt or pick up the color of your attendants' dresses by adding a few carefully placed fresh flowers to the train of your gown. Attach silk flower clusters to the shoulders of a sleeveless dress or edge your hemline with tiny, colored silk flowers, embroidered ribbon or colored bands of lace or satin. Golden seed pearls might accent the entire gown. Sew on strategically placed colored appliques or attach satin bows — perhaps toward the bottom of the gown and centered behind white lace appliques. A gingham ribbon or nosegay on a sash might accentuate the waist with a flower-decorated parasol being carried to complete the look.

Pay special attention to the back of your gown. This is one of the rare occasions when the back is as important as the front — as you walk down the aisle. For a unique touch, add your dash of color to the back — perhaps gold... a heart-shaped ribbon, a feather cluster, a belt, bow, flower, etc...

## Attendants' Fashions

Dress your wedding party so that everyone looks and feels terrific! Consider the range of budgets and bodies when selecting formalwear and dresses. You may wish to give maids and ushers a voice in the final selection. You and your groom might choose two or three men's outfits and let the ushers take a vote. You and your maids might browse through bridal magazines, shop around a bit and talk over preferences in style, color and price. Remember, your attendants' attire is the basis for your color scheme. Choose colors carefully to reflect your individual taste.

Maids may especially like clothes they will be able to wear again — from hat to shoes. For practicality, consider a long skirt with a lacy white blouse or a long halter dress with capelet or jacket.

Your maid or matron of honor may be separated from the rest of your maids by wearing a lighter shade than they, a darker shade or any contrasting color you desire. There may be a simple difference in her gown, perhaps something especially added such as a jacket, ruffle, bow, etc... You may choose to have each attendant in a different color of the same style dress with your honor attendant being singled out in another way — perhaps a different headpiece or bouquet arrangement.

Consider shades of brown and rust for fall, pastels for spring, rainbow colors for summer and jewel tones to create a dramatic winter look. Don't be afraid to coordinate "your favorite" colors. Note: Many shoe stores are able and willing to dye shoes to match your attendants' outfits.

Your flower girl may take on the look of a miniature bride or wear a dress suited to her young age made from the same fabric in the same color your attendants will be wearing or in a contrasting color. For your flower girl, you might also consider a muslin apron decorated with flowers and embroidery or a lacy pinafore.

**The Headpiece**

View a wide selection of available veils and headpieces before you make your final decision. Choose one to coordinate with your wedding day outfit as well as reflect your own personality — perhaps a lace crown headpiece with crystals and pearls, tiers of veiling and white ribbon streamers or a captivating headpiece with a long, trailing veil and a pouff of netting touched with lace medallions; perhaps a princess-look tiara interwoven with cathedral-length mantilla edged in satin or a sequin crown with tiered veiling; perhaps a wide, lacy fantasy hat or a headband of feathers and flowers or eyelet ruffles.

No matter what types of headpieces are considered for yourself or your attendants, flowers may stand alone or make a delightful addition. Perhaps it will be a halo of orange blossoms and pearls or a simple sprig of baby's breath. A floral wreath with veiling emphasizes a pretty bridal face. Consider open-crowned picture hats with flower trim, lace and ribbons. Show off a graceful neck with hair pulled up and caught in a circle of blossoms.

Think about hair combs — with bows, flowing ribbon streamers, lace pouffs or pom-poms — or, sprays of flowers to one side of the head with hat or headpiece set to the opposite side, bonnets with bouffant veiling, wide velvet ribbon headbands or straw hats donned with flowers.

A tiny lace fan or a princess tiara decorated with flowers will make an adorable headpiece for your flower girl. Or, consider decorative barrettes or combs entwined with ribbon streamers.

**Fashion Accessories**

What kind of hose should you wear? With today's fashions, you may be just as fancy as you wish about your hose. They are usually natural in shade, but you may wear fancy white or ivory lace or mesh stockings. If your dress isn't white or if you've chosen a sprinkle or color for your bridal outfit — pink organza bows or a shimmery satin mint-green bodice under white lace — then, why not wear tinted hosiery for a polished look. Colored stockings can be an evident, delicate outfit accessory. Suggest this to your maids also, coordinating everyone in an identical color.

Consider a feminine ankle bracelet or tuck and tie scented ribbons around your ankles. Glue tiny seed pearls, beads or rhinestones to your hose at the ankle to form a flower, heart or other decoration. You might attach enticing appliques of velvet or lace. Even if your dress is floor length, what a lovely added touch any one of these ideas might make to a photograph as your groom removes your garter.

Do cushion your feet with insoles for a wedding day in comfort. Should you desire to wear flat shoes, consider satin ballet slippers to which you might add a hand-painted flower or gold initial monogram. For added use, choose shoes that may be dyed after the wedding to match a special outfit. Your shoes may be especially noticeable when you lift your skirt as your groom removes your garter or as he whirls you onto the dance floor. Add a special touch — tiny satin bows attached to the ankle straps or one fresh flower from your bouquet attached to the toe of each shoe.

For that "something old", consider heirloom jewelry, your mother's or grandmother's petticoat or gloves or a lacy handkerchief that has been in the family. You may wish to coordinate a piece of heirloom lace into your new dress, reembroider an antique applique or even wear the dress that made your mother's wedding day so special.

Though there are more modern and practical ways, you may choose to utilize a dress hoop, favoring the methods of past times, to hold up the train of your dress as you dance. The train is held up as it is pulled through the hoop. The hoop rests on your left arm at the wrist — a charming touch to an old-fashioned wedding theme.

Traditionally, "something blue" is the bridal garter. If yours is not, why not wear one in your wedding colors to add one more bright touch to this special day? Simply run elastic through two pieces of stitched, satin ribbon. If you wish, add lace, maribou fur or tiny decorations of any kind. You might embroider it with hearts and flowers or your initials and wedding date. Why not make and wear more than one garter... one to throw, one to keep forever and perhaps one to pass on to someone special. Spray your garter with your wedding day fragrance.

Multiple handkerchiefs is another splendid idea. Embroider, decorate and scent three — one for yourself, one for your mother and one for his mother. Have the handkerchiefs for both mothers placed in their seats prior to the service — a pleasant little surprise awaiting their arrival. Ask your florist to incorporate your hanky into your bouquet or to fashion a wristlet for you to wear with your handkerchief and a few flowers attached to a silk ribbon to be tied around your wrist. Instead of the traditional white lace handkerchief, consider a colorful one.

You may or may not choose to carry a handkerchief that has been passed on to you, just as you may or may not choose to pass yours along — perhaps to your own daughter or to the next woman in your family to marry so that she may do the same for another bride.

You may wish to save a lacy, white handkerchief to fashion a bonnet for the "hospital-homecoming" or christening of your first child.

### Subtle Details For a Romantic Bride

If you're using elbow-length gloves or gauntlets, consider a row of flowers or pearls arranged the length of the glove. To ward off frosty fingers on the way to the church in winter, wear soft cashmere or leather gloves in any pale color or carry a cuddly, white fur muff.

To add to a softly romantic look, tie dainty sheer gloves at the wrist with satin ribbons or weave a ribbon through your hair. Wear a string of pearls bracelet or place a string of pearls across the top of your head to go with a veil or headpiece that fits nearer to the back of the head.

Concerning fragrance, wear the one loved most by your groom or the one that makes you feel at your very best — fresh, beautiful and captivating!

Your Groom —
Your Co-Star

## YOUR GROOM — YOUR CO-STAR

As soon as you have selected bridesmaids' outfits, you and your groom should contact your local formalwear specialist to view formalwear for him and his attendants. A large range of colors and styles is available.

Small details can go a long way in creating a unique look for the groom. A pleat here, a change in cut there can make a big difference. Other ideas might include fancy ruffled shirts or those with pleated or birds-eye pique fronts, velvet vests, wing-collar shirts with smaller band bow ties, studs, cufflinks, detachable dickies and curved lapels.

In full dress tailcoat, your groom might don a black top hat and white gloves to complete the look. In a tuxedo, he can personalize with cummerbund, vest and bow tie — perhaps one in attendants' colors. Color sparks up any outfit, and all it takes is a little bit — a floral boutonniere or a floral print or colored satin ascot instead of a plain tie, pocket squares or suspenders.

A dash of another fabric — for lapels, collars, pocket trimming or tie — adds shimmer to his wedding suit, so look for rich contrasts in texture as well as color — plush velvets, smooth satin, etc...

### The Bouttonniere

A single flower or cluster of flowers, perhaps backed by greenery, is the traditional accessory that your groom wears on his left lapel. What flower will he wear? With a little attention, his look can be original! Perhaps a stem of lily of the valley or a sprig of tiny flowers backed by a single green leaf. Choose flowers for attendants' lapels to coordinate with the bridesmaids' dresses.

You may wish to follow the custom of removing a flower from your bouquet and pinning it to your groom's lapel. If so, why not plan to do this when you greet him at the altar for a most sentimental touch to your day?

## Send a Surprise

Take one romantic moment to send a "surprise" to your husband-to-be. It might be a small token enclosed in a card thoughtfully expressing your feelings. Mail the card ahead so that he will receive it the day of the wedding.

Send a gift or message via a third party. His parents may "make the delivery" at breakfast the day of the wedding or his best man might deliver your "surprise" just prior to the start of the ceremony.

# Attendant Care

## ATTENDANT CARE

Feel free to modify tradition. If you or your groom would like to have two honor attendants, ask two! You might have a maid *and* a matron of honor and divide responsibilities between both. How many attendants? Just as many as you want. If you come up with more maids than groomsmen (or vice versa), pair extras two by two and have them follow your maid/usher couples. Adapt the rules to meet your needs. An usher might escort your acolyte during the recessional.

What about a pregnant attendant? Though tradition says she should excuse herself from the wedding party, if you would really like to have her, ask her if she feels able to participate. If you'd like, you might make her an honorary "organizer"or "official hostess" instead, armed with telephone numbers to see that all deliveries are on time and correct. She might also pin on corsages (order one for her, too), see that the procession begins on time and take care of putting together a "last minute survival kit".

A broken fingernail, snagged pantyhose, a ripped hem — problems no bride or member of the wedding party wants on wedding day. Your "survival kit", which might be located in the ladies room for guests as well, should include: safety pins, band-aids, hair pins, tissues, breath mints, hand towelettes, nail polish, scissors, needle and thread, comb, baby powder, tape, nail file, tampons, aspirin, etc... After the reception, pack your kit to take on your honeymoon.

You may want to include children in the wedding party as miniature bride and groom, flower girls or ring bearers. Two special children? Remember, you *can* modify tradition — perhaps two flower girls and a ring bearer or two ring bearers. Do plan to spend some time ahead of wedding day with any young children that will be participating in the ceremony. Use pictures or dolls to help explain exactly what each child will be expected to do. Together, you might devise your very own countdown calendar. Make your own "fun".

Ask young teens to serve as junior bridesmaids or junior ushers. Your ten-year-old brother may seem too old to be a ring bearer and too young to be a groomsman. Make him an honorary attendant with "special responsibilities". He might seat your mother, the groom's parents and/or grandparents and help with car decorating or any other tasks you might assign.

It may be that you wish to include your grandparents, godparents, or any "special someone" in your wedding plans. They might:

> design your invitation or program cover
> help address invitations
> make wedding day accessories
> help organize gifts
> meet out-of-town guests at the airport, train or bus terminal and see them to their lodging
> be "wedding chauffeurs" — to run special wedding errands
> make food (from old family recipes) (special hors d'oeuvres)
> light candles before the procession
> read a welcoming prayer or special poem
> hand out Mass books before the service or Yarmulkes at a Jewish ceremony
> distribute rice packets
> serve punch or pass out pieces of wedding cake
> tend to the guest book at the reception
> announce the special events of the reception such as when you will be cutting the cake, throwing the bouquet, etc...

Show your appreciation to friends and family members who have agreed to be in your wedding. You might have someone announce the names of the entire wedding party as you enter your reception hall or after you have all been seated at the head table.

If many of your attendants will be coming from out-of-town, consider photocopying helpful information such as a schedule of week-end events, addresses and telephone numbers and a detailed city (or area) map.

What about pre-nuptial parties? Why not get your group together before the wedding? You might treat both male and female attendants to a fruit and cheese party, a poolside barbecue or a cheese or chocolate fondue party. For contagious fun on a cold winter's day, try reviving a delightful turn-of-the-century tradition: pulling taffy. Be creative. Show your appreciation by holding your very own ice cream social. Serve ice cream and platters of fresh fruits such as strawberries, raspberries, pineapple spears and banana slices. Don't forget the nuts and whipped cream. Set out an assortment of glasses and bowls and invite your attendants to build their own sundaes.

Why not tie a progressive party into your plans? Start as a group in one location for cocktails and hors d'oeuvres. Advance to another for a meal — perhaps a buffet dinner, and to yet another for dessert. Share a meaningful moment at each location: announcement, toast, future plans or the exchange of "special engagement gifts" between you and your groom. Sound like fun? It will be and it's a chance for everyone to get acquainted and contribute any suggestions well before the wedding.

Thank your attendants at a bridesmaids' lunch or brunch. Prepare a special meal. For example, have a pasta party, serve fresh crepes or a soup and salad bar arrangement. Offer champagne and a pretty cake so your maids can toast you. Bake the cake full of surprises — a charm wrapped in wax paper baked into each slice or bake in the "traditional thimble". The one who finds the thimble in her slice will be the next one to marry.

Remember each person who helps you with a small gift and a personal "thank you" note. Say thank you to your attendants with personable, practical gifts. Use your imagination! You are close to the members of the wedding party so you should be familiar with their personal tastes. A gift that relates to their hobby perhaps, — sewing? needlepoint? photography? sports? theater? etc... Perhaps a gift made by hand with special care. Crochet a lacy purse for each maid or sew them from velvet or satin. Consider handmade or wicker baskets filled with personal items for each of your maids. You might include powder, lotion, perfume, sachets, etc... Fill fabric scraps with bath salts to make sachets. The scent will last a long time and the bath salts will always be usable.

For children, consider tickets to a special event in town, an engraved trophy, a locket or a characteristic doll — one that is dressed like you or one that's dressed like her. A final note regarding gifts — wrap them brightly, creatively!

Music
A Most Important
Ingredient

# MUSIC — A MOST IMPORTANT INGREDIENT

It's your day and whether it will be tradition or modern, you can individualize even more with music. Let your music set the tone and reflect your personality. You might wish to seek the advice of friends involved in music. Do keep in mind throughout your planning that music should support and never upstage the ceremonial elements.

You may wish to involve your friends and family in this aspect of your wedding. A friend who plays guitar? Invite him (or her) to play at the wedding as a solo or with voice, flute, piano or organ. Invite friends who can sing well to participate. The more personalized you make your ceremony, the more meaningful it will be. If you want to involve your attendants more fully in the proceedings, why not ask each of them to choose a musical selection?

To precede the ceremony, consider a trio of violinists playing as guests filter in, a soft prelude to last half an hour — perhaps broken mid-way by the first solo or, perhaps a soft medley of songs. Many couples choose a particular piece to be played as their parents are being seated to help serve as a "cue" to wedding party members that the ceremony is about to begin. This may be a good opportunity to utilize mom and dad's musical choice or, perhaps a song that was played during their wedding ceremony.

The wedding marches of Wagner and Mendelssohn are beautiful, but there are many other marches to choose from as well. You may even consider replacing the bridal march with your entire church choir in song. If you're planning to have a large number of attendants, or if the aisle is long, consider using two processionals.

As you decide upon songs for your wedding ceremony, do make sure that lyrics say what you want to be said. Include at least one song with special meaning to you and your groom. Choose a meditative solo, perhaps a favorite hymn, to follow the solemn taking of vows; a joyous recessional and perhaps a festive tune to be played as guests are leaving the church. Wedding musicians will generally be willing to purchase any special music you want, and most are glad to have the opportunity to expand their own repertoire. You may wish to list your musical selections in your printed program or have lyrics printed and available for a song (or songs) that will be part of your ceremony. Your soloist or clergyman could invite guests to join in the singing.

**More Musical Considerations**

1. If you like the sound of brass, include it. Trumpet or cornet would add a distinctive note.
2. Consider harp, flute or accordian.
3. Violin and flute are good in combination.
4. Consider two or three trombones and one cornet.
5. Choose organ with string, brass or woodwind soloist.
6. Consider an instrumental or vocal ensemble.

Etiquette rules are adamant against the bride and/or groom singing at their own wedding... but it's up to you. Instead of singing live, you may consider pre-recording one or two special songs to be played during the ceremony.

Music at your reception? Create a pleasing atmosphere. A trio serves well for most receptions, but if your budget and location allow for it, select a band with the sound you want — from strolling musicians to rock to polka to a 40's Big Band sound, or even Scottish bagpipes. Consider a group of accomplished performers located through your local high school, college, music teachers' association or musicians' union. Arrange to hear them perform ahead of time to be sure you will be happy with their sound. For a "touch of class", hire the symphony and professional singers — expensive, but unforgettable!

As an alternative to "live" music, consider the use of records and tapes. You might create 60 or 90 minute cassette tapes with the musical variety you desire.

Capture Memorable
Moments Forever

# CAPTURE MEMORABLE MOMENTS FOREVER

Bridal photography should be well-planned as your wedding photos will be your most treasured mementos. They capture all of the emotion, joy, happiness and excitement of one of the most memorable occasions in your lifetime.

Select a reputable photographer to take your engagement and wedding photos. The engagement picture to be sent to newspapers might include your groom as well.

Do check with friends who have utilized the services of any photographer you may be considering. The most popular package offered by a professional photographer is an album of posed formals and unposed candids, plus possibly a few special effects pictures. Special effects pictures are becoming increasingly popular. If your photographer doesn't openly offer any to you, discuss possibilities with him.

For example, double exposures prove interesting, perhaps over stained glass windows or some other equally dramatic background such as a pretty statue, decorated doorway or anything you might suggest. You may request that a picture of you and your groom taken during the bridal dance be centered over a background of sheet music — from one of your wedding songs.

"Misty" pictures are available which lend a dreamy appearance to a meditative pose. Another special effect idea combines two pictures — again a double exposure: the top half of the "total picture" might be the bride and groom angled forward and looking down at the bottom half of the "total picture" which might be a ceremonial scene inclusive of the entire wedding party as the bride and groom are saying their vows.

Silhouettes create an attractive effect. For example, a full-color picture of the head of the bride or the groom might appear within a dark outlined silhouette of the head of the other (bride or groom). Interesting pictures can be created by combining photography and lighting effects.

Candles can be made to look like stars and ceiling lights can create the effect of colorful prisms.

Work closely with your photographer in defining your choices of pictures. A few days before the wedding, select a person from your family and from the groom's family to assist the photographer. Your wedding contacts can be on hand to locate special guests, relatives and close friends at the reception.

You may take it for granted that you'll get the usual pictures of your cake, flowers and the reception, but if you want to be certain that your hand-made cake top, wicker wall decorations and floral topiary tree head table decorations are included, be sure to tell your photographer ahead of time. You might instruct your photographer to capture each guest on film and then send a print as a memento with each thank you note.

Most photographers have checklists for you to view and from which to make your choices prior to the wedding, but you need to remember that *any* unique or unusual touches you are adding to your wedding day need to be specifically mentioned.

A suggestion: What about videotaping or filming your entire ceremony?

**Before the Wedding — A Photographic Note**

At his bachelor party, your shower or any other pre-nuptial party, provide one or two instant cameras. Let the guests take the pics. The candids will let you and your fiance know what went on at each other's special party. You might use these pictures as placecards at your rehearsal dinner or the wedding reception.

# Your Flowers
# A Bouquet of Ideas

# YOUR FLOWERS — A BOUQUET OF IDEAS

For centuries, flowers have symbolized the wonderful wedding sentiments of love and joy. The key to selecting the perfect flowers for your wedding is to work with a reputable florist, within your budget.

Regardless of the type of wedding you have, no doubt you will carry a bridal bouquet. This tradition has endured. Choose your bouquet to complement you and your dress. If the wedding gown you've chosen is from one of the romanticized eras of days gone by, your flowers should also portray that mood. Basket designs and colonial nosegays best capture this old-fashioned feeling and for an added antique flair, you might consider incorporating dried blossoms and heirloom lace. Not only will they give the design old-time charm, but also allow it to serve as a lasting keepsake.

For those who have selected a more contemporary look — flowing hooded gowns, simple designs or sleek jersey styles — perhaps long-stemmed roses or other flowers tied with streaming ribbons or airy clusters of blossoms designed with their natural stems exposed to create a loose, garden-picked look. They can be hand-held or arm-cradled. For the traditional bride — dressed in yards of delicate lace and veiling with appliques and rows of decorative beads — the majestic cascade (round or heart-shaped) or crescent bouquets offer elegance and sophistication.

To personalize, feel free to vary. For example, consider a single flower. The Calla lily will complement the tall woman. A sprig of apple blossom or a single long-stemmed rose accentuated with baby's breath may also be considerations. Any one flower of the bride's choice might be surrounded by full, decorative foliage. A single large green leaf, hand-held and decorated with flowers carefully placed might complete your look. A single flower may also be worn on a band as a choker or pendant around the neck.

Consider a wrist bouquet. Small flowers such as

miniature roses and carnations form a dainty heart-shaped cascade extending down the side of the hand. Incorporate baby's breath and dried rosebuds. The wrist corsage is smaller than the wrist bouquet and is generally shaped like a round puff.

Add flowers (and/or feathers, maribou fur) to a lacy white fan to create a pretty backdrop for a cascading bouquet. Consider natural wicker fans for your attendants decorated with straw flowers and wheat for a perfect fall wedding.

Perhaps the classic wreath may be your style. The wreath, not just for the holiday season, is an assortment of fine-textured flowers, greens and ribbon woven into the shape of a circle (or heart) and held in the hands of the bride or her attendants. Consider a chain of dried rosebuds strung like popcorn with tiny bows to create a delicate-looking wreath or accent greens with roses, wild grasses, lilies and clover; perhaps baby's breath and statice.

Wedding flowers with a lighter feel? How about a circlet of delicate orchids and trailing vines or a whimsical floral boa, imaginative, perfect for an outdoor or informal wedding.

Other alternatives to the hand-held bouquet include a slender staff of ribbon-wrapped flowers or a decorated parasol. The parasol is charming — open, or closed with flowers peeping out toward the handles and trailing over the sides. Ask your florist to tie a ribbon around the spokes to help keep parasols shut during the ceremony. At the reception, parasols carried by maids may be opened to create an arch as you and your groom enter. A wrist corsage or a wrist bouquet might also be worn by a bride or maid carrying a parasol.

The hand-held muff is another alternative — of lace and flowers, airy for spring or, of velvet or fur for winter or of matching gown fabric for anytime. For a formal wedding, the bride may consider a prayer book decorated with a few flowers chosen from her own garden and a four-leaf clover or tiny silver horseshoe included for good luck. For her attendants, perhaps baskets of flowers mixed with clusters of grapes and berries or spray-painted pinecones mixed with blossoms.

Gold-touched bouquets add sophistication and elegance. Simply spray paint silk flowers (or leaves) with gold spray paint and ask your florist to arrange them with greenery or add a few real flowers such as carnations or roses to the bouquet. You may wish to replace the traditional white ribbon streamers that generally flow from wedding bouquets with golden streamers or feminine-looking chains decorated with a few flowers and a bit of greenery or a dangling lei of miniature flowers.

The bride may wish to tie "flowers of significance" into her bouquet. Perhaps your favorite flowers are those representing important months such as the month of your wedding, the month the two of you met, your birthday, his birthday, etc... To add beautiful color, why not individualize the bouquets of your attendants by incorporating flowers of their birth months into each bouquet.

Select bouquet "ingredients" according to what they represent:

Orange Blossom ... a bridal flower since ancient times; is a symbol of good luck, happiness, fruitfulness

Iris ............... symbolizes good health

Periwinkle,
Jasmine,
Lily of the Valley ... symbolize happiness

Baby's Breath ..... symbolizes fertility

Rose ............. ancient Greeks regarded the rose as queen of flowers, and considered it an emblem of beauty and happiness; symbolizes love, joy and beauty

53

| | |
|---|---|
| Lily . . . . . . . . . . . . . . . | favored by the Greeks as an emblem of perfect purity and innocence |
| Heather,<br>Sweet Basil . . . . . . . . | symbolize fortune |
| Apple Blossoms . . . | symbolize good fortune and a promise of better things to come |
| Myrtle . . . . . . . . . . . . . | perpetual freshness symbolizes constancy in duty and affection |
| Rosemary . . . . . . . . . | reflects lovers' commitment and fidelity |
| Olive & Laurel<br>Leaves . . . . . . . . . . . . | symbolize plenty of virtue |

## More Floral Ideas For Brides

Why not scent bouquets — peppermint for spring, strawberry for summer or, include fragrant lavender in your bouquet? For a sentimental touch, carry a bouquet identical to your mother's or tie the stems of your bouquet with lace hand-crocheted by an aunt or grandmother.

If you include a non-flowering item in your bouquet — perhaps a sprig of rosemary, myrtle or ivy, why not pass it along to the next bride in your family. Your "something old" might be a flower or vine taken from your grandmother's garden or houseplant, then woven into your bouquet by your florist. Many old ethnic customs invite luck with flowers. A German bride would wind flax around her garter, while a Roman bride sewed verbena into honeymoon bed pillows (you could tuck some in your ring pillow).

For a lasting, living memory, grow pretty rose bushes from your bouquet. Make sure roses have stem of 4-6 inches. Prepare cuttings by snipping off the flowers and slitting open the nodes on the stems. Dip each cutting into a hormone rooting powder. Fill small pots with one-third each of sand, vermiculite and peat moss, and gently press in cuttings. Water thoroughly and cover tightly with plastic wrap. Watch for signs of life (about 3-4 weeks). You can follow the same steps with carnations, chrysanthemums, even bouquet greens such as ivy.

A bouquet to throw? If you're carrying a fan, you might throw a wrist corsage or floral wreath. If you're not planning a separate bouquet to throw, think about having your flowers made into a "breakaway" bouquet: the concealed center or bottom trail (if it's a cascade) could be removed by you for a lasting keepsake. Or, remove a few flowers yourself before throwing, perhaps to form a corsage. You might combine silk with fresh flowers, removing only the silk.

If yours is a loosely-tied bouquet, toss each of your maids a sprig or, divy up your bouquet and give one blossom to each single guest. If your bouquet is not loosely-tied, you might give each attendant a cutting from it. Should you decide to skip bouquet-throwing altogether, you and your groom might choose to surprise a couple (perhaps the next ones to be married) with a formal presentation of the garter and bouquet.

## Flowers In The Sanctuary

The creative bride may wish to design her own altar flower arrangement grouping flowers or plants by using baskets or vases. Picture clusters of colorful tulips or carnations banking the altar. You might incorporate flower-accented candles. For a Jewish ceremony, order a flowered huppah entwined with ivy vines.

Ask your florist to add to the aisle runner — perhaps chains of flowers along both sides or tiny flower clusters or big colorful bows equally spaced the length of the aisle runner. Consider a colored aisle runner (if possible) — perhaps a blue one for the blue and white "Blessed Mother Wedding" or a red one for the red and white "Sacred Heart Wedding" or one to match your total color scheme.

Consider wicker half-baskets filled with flowers or big satin bows to serve as pew markers or, attach lilac clusters to pew posts to symbolize youthful love.

## At The Reception

For reception decorating, you might buy flowers in bulk from your florist and arrange them yourself. Try vases of tall dogwood or forsythia branches, autumn leaves, pine boughs, or whatever is in season at the time. Rent tall plants from a nursery. Potted plants might enhance the reception atmosphere adding freshness and warmth. When the reception is in a house, it is thoughtful to put flowers in every room that will be used — including the bathroom. If you can use the same flowers that were used during the ceremony, you'll reduce costs significantly. Bridesmaids' bouquets should be placed along the outer edge of the head table to form a beautiful, colorful border.

Do think ahead... to the freedom of flowers to *wear* at the reception. Keep the look and lovely scent of fresh flowers near you. Switch to a wrist corsage, hairflowers, too — for dancing, greeting guests and having fun.

## More For the Reception
## And Other Considerations

1. Decorative topiary forms are becoming increasingly popular. These forms are stuffed with moss and planted with creeping myrtle, ivy or any small leaf vine. Flowers may be incorporated. Consider round or heart-shaped, bells or swan-shaped forms — even a floral carousel.

2. Imagine the hotel or country club pool with floating gardenias for each guest to take home as a special memento.

3. Include a small tree in your floral plans. Plant it afterward where you can watch it grow along with your

marriage. You might include miniature Christmas trees decorated with roses, strings of floral buds or berries with novelty decorations such as bells and lovebirds.

4. Include greens. For example, lemon leaves, huckleberry and scented eucalyptus leaves.

5. Consider wedding terrariums as reception decorations.

6. Place a floral arch or canopy at the entrance to the church or reception hall.

7. Tree branches decorated with silk flowers are a unique, decorative idea.

8. Use chains of flowers or hanging baskets.

9. For an outdoor wedding, decorate the garden gate, trellis, fence, gazebo or whatever is appropriate. Outline a path in rose petals.

10.For lighting, consider stringing colonial lanterns. Include flower-filled baskets.

11.Consider big, colorful tissue-paper flowers for the reception, or set out delicate silk flowers in napkin-wrapped soda bottles; tie with skinny ribbons.

12.Cluster small pots of flowering plants to form one centerpiece. Group small cacti and jades in shallow pots; pack with moss and tuck candles at edges.

13.Don't forget about fruits, vegetables and herbs. With a little imagination, they too, can be formed into elegant, sophisticated centerpieces.

14.Bring a bit of the outdoors in. Drill holes in small wooden logs and fill the holes with floral stems.

15.Set small plants at each place setting as favors for guests. How about forget-me-nots or white clover?

16. If tent canopies are used, ask your florist for help with ideas for wrapping the support poles — ribbon streamers, fabric, flowers and trailing ivy, crepe paper, etc... The space at the center of the canopy is a perfect place to hang balloon bouquets, baskets, banners, macramed wind chimes, etc...

17. The simplicity of grapevines lends itself to many kinds of accents — wreaths or baskets decorated (or filled) with fruit, rosehips, evergreens, pinecones, nuts, ribbons, etc...

18. Don't overlook fragrance. Bundles of cinnamon sticks in pinecone baskets or old-fashioned pomander balls — kumquats, oranges or lemons studded with whole cloves.

19. Consider hawaiian leis: for reception decorating, attendants or guests.

20. Corsages and boutonnieres make those who can't be in the bridal party feel like a special part of your wedding too. So be sure to include not only your parents and grandparents, but also brothers, sisters, other key guests and those helping with the wedding arrangements.

21. Add a perky nosegay to the top of your cake or ask your baker to imbed a tiny vase in the cake's center to hold a few miniature flowers. You might opt for fresh flowers on each layer and/or matching garland to encircle its base.

22. Brighten the buffet table, gift and guest-book tables with fresh, colorful floral dishes.

23. Don't forget your going away corsage.

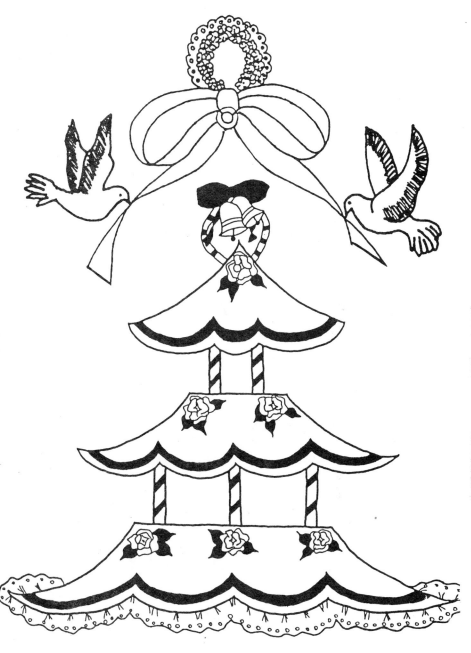

Wedding Cake

# WEDDING CAKE

The cake and "something bubbly" with which to toast the bridal couple, are the only two necessary wedding reception "ingredients".

Discuss unique cake ideas with your baker or caterer. For a touch out of the ordinary, place a running fountain within a pagoda- or gazebo-shaped cake. Consider several smaller cakes with yellow, chocolate or other flavored batters, grouped or tiered together to create the look you want; or choose a distinct, "high-spirited" flavoring. Perhaps a splash of rum in the frosting of a dark cake, a fruit liqueur in the filling of an otherwise traditional cake or a touch of a spirit liqueur in the batter. Taste samples if you can. Ask your fiance to sample with you or, better still, invite your attendants and friends to a pre-wedding cake-testing party.

A small, at-home wedding reception with true old-fashioned flavor offers the perfect opportunity to express personal taste and style not only in preparing the food and arranging the flowers, but in baking the cake as well. For decorations you can start making well in advance, consider hand-modeling dainty doves, bells, flowers and other creative trimmings out of marzipan. The cake itself can be baked ahead, frozen and frosted a day or so before the wedding.

Consider cake shape. You may wish to cut into a heart-shaped cake or a carousel-shaped cake. Or, get the personal look you want and save money by decorating a smaller 3-tiered wedding cake made, perhaps, of bell shapes. You might use this cake for the cutting ceremony and photographs and serve guests sheet cake.

Decorate your cake with flair. Add touches of color to frosting to coordinate with your total color scheme. Fresh flowers are a lovely complement. You might add bows or ribbons, perhaps one tiny red one... symbolic of happiness. Choose a cake top reflective of your personality — novelty, traditional or even one of hand-blown glass. If you have the time, visit local craft stores for ideas on available novelty decorations as well as on making your own cake top.

Cut that first slice of wedding cake with a special knife. Serve it with a matching server. You may wish to purchase these items with special china or pearl handles or purchase them in your sterling pattern. As a special tribute, use mom's and dad's cake knife. Simply add a new ribbon, a few flowers and your names and wedding date for a meaningful keepsake.

As you and your groom enjoy that "first bite" of wedding cake, make a special wish together or a special promise to each other. Make the first cut into the top layer so that as you remember your wedding day one year from now, you will remember this particularly meaningful moment.

If you have the caterer pack the cake in wedding cake bags or boxes for guests to take home, you can place them on a table to be picked up as guests leave, or have them brought around by a special wedding helper. Boxes may be white, silver or any shade that matches your colors. Decorate if desired. Tie with a scented ribbon and attach a fresh or silk flower.

Consider saving individual pieces of wedding cake to share together for anniversaries 2 through 5.

### The Groom's Cake — An Old Tradition

The groom's cake is *his* cake — so he can be the one to decide the flavor, shape and decorations. Any flavor is appropriate so long as it differs from the bride's cake. Fruitcake is traditional, but other choices might include cheesecake, banana cake, nut cake, spice cake or carrot cake, all scrumptious with cream cheese frosting. You may even consider baked alaska or a decorated ice cream cake if it can be kept cold.

Perhaps a cake that's horseshoe-shaped, bell-shaped, Bible-shaped or heart-shaped would be his preference.

Another variation: the groom's cake can be the upper-most layer of the bride's cake. If the groom's cake is the top tier, you might freeze it for your first anniversary celebration.

Decorations? Perhaps a meaningful quotation or an ornament to represent his hobby or a shared interest.

If you serve the groom's cake at the reception, cut it together also and feed each other a piece.

*Chapter P.S.*
*There is no reason why any of the ideas suggested for the groom's cake, could not be used for the bride's cake instead!*

# — Notes to Myself —

# Candles –
## Mystical and Impressive

## CANDLES — MYSTICAL AND IMPRESSIVE

The symbolic candle is a mystical, impressive addition to your celebration of unity. Candles might be burning as guests are seated, lit just before the mother of the bride is seated or lit by honored guests or an usher during the ceremony.

Ask a special friend or relative to serve as an acolyte (candle lighter). He or she would precede the bridal party down the aisle lighting candles in whatever scheme you have them placed — perhaps on pedestals at the ends of several pews on either side of the aisle, in candelabrum on either side of the altar or in arrangements of hanging, flower-accented baskets. Check with your local rental center for a unique candelabra — perhaps heart-shaped. *Special Note:* It's possible to rent just about anything — from tables to goblets, to dessert plates to silver to linens to hanging lanterns, etc....

Group glowing candles around the ceremony area. You and your groom might take lit tapers from each side of the altar and together light a "50-Year Unity Candle" in the center, or after you have said your vows, your parents and his might approach the altar holding large family candles from which you and your groom each light a taper prior to your lighting the unity candle. Another option might be for your respective families to light family candles on either side of the altar prior to the ceremony. You and your groom might hold these family candles joined together so that two lights form one bright, radiant flame.

Show the merging of two families. Each of you might escort your parents (or mothers only) to the altar allowing them to use separate candles to light a unity flame.

Involve your wedding attendants by giving each of them a single candle. Prior to the taking of the vows, allow the maid of honor and the best man to light their candles from a lit taper on the altar. They then would light the remaining attendants' candles to form a "radiance" around the two of you. You may want only your brides-maids to carry candles or have them carry pretty lanterns decorated with flowers and greenery to match your color scheme.

Have your clergyman light candles for you and your groom. You may then carry them in the recessional, or you may light candles for each of your attendants as well so that all of you may carry lit candles in the recessional.

At a winter wedding, allow each guest to light a candle as he leaves the church. Ask guests to make a little hollow in the snow, setting the candle inside so that the flame is protected from the wind. The group of candles will create a flattering, romantic glow as well as a pretty "scenery setting" for pictures.

Decorate large candles with lilacs, ferns, greenery, birds of paradise and palm leaves. Use colored bows and baby's breath to decorate smaller ones. Roll candles in a warm towel and add glitter. Consider scented candles — vanilla, strawberry, cinnamon, mint, etc... A holiday wed-ding might suggest candles entwined with holly sprigs, shiny berries and deep red velvet ribbon.

Illuminate the reception hall entrance with real candles set in sconces. At the reception, place a candle on the guest book table and candelabrum on the bridal table. Or, the bridal table might feature one large white candle in the center with white votive candles in glass holders at each place setting. Choose a specific area (perhaps the guest book table or cake table) and group flowers with layers of scented votive candles to create a dramatic "garden".

Allow your guests to dine by candlelight or have a spe-cial candlelight dance. Consider floating candles in decorated goldfish bowls, wine glasses or brandy snifters. Even more unique? Consider ball-shaped can-dles in tall candlesticks, white dove-shaped candles in porcelain holders, or imagine groups of painted twigs, illuminated with tiny clear lights and set in crystal vases.

Plant your candles. Place a sprouting of candles in plain clay (or decorated) pots (safe in sand). Fill in with greens and/or flowers. To form unique centerpieces, mix candles and fruit. For example, pierce highly polished apples and put in tiny tapers. Stem with tiny satin bows. Or, create a lasting wreath. Use a cluster of tiny tapers or center with one big candle for a mellow glow.

Use strands of tiny white Christmas tree lights and rent lanterns to illuminate an outdoor reception. Gardens can be lit by candlelight. Use yard-high metal stakes fitted on top with metal saucers and small hurricane lamps that shelter a votive light. Imagine an outdoor reception lit by torches or suspended chandeliers or create a unique, warm glow with bag lights. To make bag lights, simply weigh paper lunch bags with sand and place a taper in the center.

# — Notes to Myself —

"Today...
Tomorrow...
And Always"

# Your Ceremony

# YOUR CEREMONY

## Planning

It helps a lot if you can attend and observe a wedding in your church, temple or synagogue. You'll see how it all happens, and you will have a better idea of what questions to ask. Talk to your clergyman about practical ceremony arrangements and ways to pattern your ceremony to your individual tastes and desires within the confines of any established rules.

Plan your wedding on a date that's meaningful to you. Perhaps the anniversary of your first date, your birthday, your parents' or grandparents' anniversary, etc... Have a part of the ceremony delivered in the native language of your forefathers. You might choose just a prayer or native ballad with translations printed in a wedding program. Observe a few "old country" wedding customs. If you don't know what they are, ask your librarian, grandparents or clergy for help.

You might choose to say your vows at a special site you love. Perhaps in your own home or in your backyard under a tent awning with raised platform; perhaps in the churchyard or in the park, at a country club or local inn, aboard a houseboat or at a historic landmark site. Or, rent a spectacular environment for the day... the botanical gardens?

Did your best friend recently get engaged? Is your future sister-in-law planning to be married soon? You may consider a double wedding. It's a way of celebrating the close bonds between friends and in the case of two members of the family, one double wedding can cut down on the expense of holding two separate weddings.

## The Arrival

For a formal or semi-formal wedding, you may wish to pamper yourself and arrive in a chauffeured limousine. It's exciting, fun and a rare treat. Creative brides have also arrived at the church on time in antique cars, sleighs and even horse-drawn carriages.

## The Processional

While the Christian bride traditionally makes her entrance on the arm of her father and meets her groom at the altar, the Jewish bride and groom are escorted down the aisle by both families, a custom others may adopt. If the clergy asks, "Who gives this woman to be married?" your father might answer "Her mother and I." Others may also adopt the Jewish custom of making grandparents a part of the processional.

Some couples have modified the customary Christian procession in another way. Instead of the usual entrance, the clergyman meets the bridal party at the door and either precedes the attendants or leads the bride accompanied by her parents and the groom escorted by his father and mother, down the aisle to the sanctuary. Those favoring such an arrangement maintain that it indicates in a more effective fashion the gift of son or daughter to the prospective bride and groom.

If you opt for the traditional entrance, share a meaningful moment with your father before you begin your "walk down the aisle". You might give him a small gift or a letter expressing personal sentiments to be read after the wedding. As you reach the altar area, you might choose to make a presentation to your mother, perhaps a single long-stemmed rose with a lace hanky, a special poem you have written, a prayer book or any thoughtful, fitting item. You might present the same item to the mother of your groom as well — at the same time or after the taking of the vows.

The traditional entrance with the bride on her father's left arm might be modified (with the consent of the clergy) to have the bride on her father's right side instead. This arrangement might be more appealing in that it brings the bride right to the left side of the groom and it eliminates the fact that the bride's father generally has to step back and walk around the train to take his seat.

## Service

Meet with your clergyman before choosing Scripture selections. You can use Scripture in a variety of ways. Ask a close friend to read a passage, or have a dramatic reading with all of the wedding party (or your family members) taking part. One way to include all guests is to have a responsive reading between clergyman and congregation. If you are writing out your service in a wedding program, include all the words to the responses to make it easier for your guests to join in. A bride and groom might speak Scripture "vows" of commitment just before their wedding vows.

Your ceremony — when you vow to be husband and wife — is one of life's most special times. Consider writing your own vows or mix traditional vows with a modern statement of your love. You might include an excerpt from a favorite song or poem. For an added touch, turn around and say your vows facing the congregation or use a microphone in an effort to more fully share the moment with your guests.

You might have married guests renew their vows after yours or perhaps just your parents and his and other married family members might step forward to renew their vows.

Incorporate symbolism in some way into your ceremony. For example, a Bible, symbolic of faith; a wreath for the bright future; rosemary for loyalty, etc... As you join hands, cover them with a white handkerchief or encircle both wrists with a wristlet or wreath of flowers — symbolic of love and unity. Ask if it is possible to have the church bells rung after you say your vows. Consider having two bells rung before you say your vows and one after you are pronounced man and wife.

Just before the groom slips the ring on your finger, it's traditional to hand your bouquet to your honor attendant, who will be standing to your left. If you'd like to include your mother in the ceremony, have her hold it instead. It will be easy for her to step forward. You take it back just as the recessional begins.

In the Catholic ceremony, participate in the joyous "sign of peace". You and your groom may go down the entire aisle (or partway) exchanging a handshake or kiss with some or all of your guests.

Wedding memories are usually captured in beautiful, but silent photographs. For an extra-special memento, tape record your ceremony and those special reception moments, too.

## Lifting The Face Veil

Years ago, the veil was solely a symbol of youth and virginity. It was lifted after the bride was legally wed. You may choose to observe this tradition now. After you have been pronounced husband and wife, either your honor attendant or your groom would lift the veil back from your face so that you can share that very first kiss that begins your life as a married couple.

You might decide to have it raised earlier in the ceremony or have it raised from the start. If your father is giving you away, allow him to lift it before he takes his seat. You could put back the veil yourself as you turn to your groom to say your vows or your maid of honor could lift it before handing you your groom's ring. Discuss this aspect of planning with your clergy.

## Afterward

Hold hands and be sure to smile as you and your groom walk back up the aisle as man and wife. As people pass through the receiving line, have a special helper pass out rice packets or rose petals or perhaps a single flower to each guest.

For a friendly feeling outdoors, have everyone stand behind you in a semicircle, then turn around after the vows and hold your receiving line right there.

Designate official "wedding cars" for transportation to the reception with big white bows and make plans for getting guests from the ceremony to the reception. First, make sure the ushers can *tell* people how to get there. Also, think about having the ring bearer and/or flower girl hand out rolled-and-ribboned maps to guests on their way out. Ask your local automobile association or chamber of commerce for maps of your area or draw your own. Or, you might print directions on the back of your wedding program. If you live in a small town, tie ribbons on trees as markers along the route to the reception.

# — Notes to Myself —

# Champagne
## and
## "The Toast"

## CHAMPAGNE AND "THE TOAST"

When it comes to drinking champagne, there is no finer occasion than a wedding. For a dramatic effect, serve champagne from eyecatching oversized bottles ranging from magnums (2 bottles) to salmanazars (12 bottles in one). You may wish to purchase a silver marriage cup from which both bride and groom drink at the same time, or purchase reception toasting glasses in your crystal pattern. Tie colorful ribbons around the stems.

Perhaps you might float orange blossoms in full champagne glasses or add "the eating of silver almond candies" to the toasting celebration. Add fruit for an elegant touch. Consider placing a melon ball, strawberry or another type of berry in each glass or frost tiny bunches of grapes by dipping them first into the champagne and then into sugar before hanging them over the side of each glass.

The coupe de Mariage ceremony, an ancient French custom, starts the wedding breakfast with the bride and groom's toast to each other. Best man calls for attention. The groom says "To Us" or "To Our Life Together".

Participate in the old French custom (where toasting comes from) by placing a square of toast in the bottom of the goblets to be used by your groom and yourself. You must finish the drink to get the toast and legend has it that the one who finishes first will rule the household.

Following the "reception toast", traditionally proposed by the best man, both bride and groom might rise to speak a few words of welcome and thanks. You may even propose a "thank-you toast" to your parents for "all their love and support".

Include champagne in your pre-nuptial festivities — perhaps an intimate, pre-wedding candlelight dinner for your parents. Toast close friends at a champagne shower or share a private toast with your bridesmaids and ushers after the wedding rehearsal to celebrate good cheer and good feelings.

After the wedding use your reception glasses for candy dishes or flower arrangements or make them into candle holders.

Non-alcoholic bubbly? You can toast with Martinelli's Gold Medal Sparkling Cider. A delightful non-alcoholic beverage, the sparkling cider has all the character of the "real thing" including extra-dry taste. Comes in traditional green champagne bottles (distributed by Hadden House Foods).

# Wedding Reception
## Food and Drink

## WEDDING RECEPTION
## FOOD AND DRINK

Talk with your caterer well ahead of your scheduled day to learn what different kinds of services can be provided and what additional special touches he/she may be able to add. Many of the following suggestions could be tied into plans for bridal showers and/or pre-nuptial parties as well.

For hors d'oeuvres, hot and cold, bite-sized finger food is best. For appetizers, consider assorted cheeses with sliced apples and nuts, chicken livers wrapped in bacon, cucumber finger sandwiches, deviled eggs, stuffed mushroom caps, cream cheese pinwheels, marinated artichoke hearts and mushrooms, pickled herring, crab puffs, miniature stuffed crepes, fresh fruit compote and crisp raw vegetables with a guacamole dip.

Fruits and vegetables add color and are least expensive when purchased in season. Think about carved watermelons or baskets of fresh fruit and vegetables. Those fruit baskets you've admired in restaurants can be easily accomplished with the v-cut knife. Insert the knife all around the middle of an orange, tomato, melon or grapefruit; the fruit then separates into two halves, each with a serrated edge. Serve these distinctive halves as is, or use them with the pulp scooped out, to serve vegetables, fresh fruit, cranberry sauce, ice cream, sherbet, etc...

Is your first course soup? If the group is not too large, consider serving it in oversized wine goblets for a touch of elegance. Interesting food tables can add to the festivities and special garnishes can make even the simplest foods impressive. Use these "gadgets" to make food prettier:

1. The miniature ice cream scoop (about 1-inch in diameter) adds elegance. Tiny scoops of a variety of sherbets in a wine glass make a lovely rainbow dessert. Special Note: Don't forget about the use of ice cream in the summer for sundaes, punch, etc...

The scoop also makes melon balls, potato balls, butter balls, etc....

2. The scallop cutter makes attractive, crinkle-cut vegetables and is ideal for preparing raw vegetables to serve with dip — carrots, cucumbers, zuccini, etc... Canned, jellied cranberry sauce also looks extra special when crinkle-cut.

3. The radish cutter makes lovely radish roses with just a squeeze of the handle. Leave them in ice water for a little while and the petals will open even more.

4. Tiny cookie cutters (called decorative cutters or canape cutters) can be used to cut vegetables, cheeses, cold luncheon meats and firm fruits to add a decorative touch to molded salads, soups, dessert, etc...

5. Those lovely curls of butter you've seen in fine restaurants are easily achieved with the uncomplicated butter curl. Simply pull it across a stick of butter. Or, use little butter molds. These are inexpensive and can be purchased in such shapes as a pineapple, wheat stalk, swan or bell. Have your caterer decorate regular butter pats with dainty blue violets to let your reception guests know that your love is forever.

The use of a champagne fountain (also for wine or punch) can add a lovely touch to your wedding reception. Talk to your caterer to find out about renting one. Dry ice in or around the fountain (or your punch bowl) will bubble and steam dramatically. Encircle the fountain base with a floral garland, a hand-made garland of white feathers and crepe paper or scattered flowers.

An ice sculpture can be purely decorative or it can serve as a cool setting for champagne bottles, fruit salad, vegetables, shrimp or caviar — shapes could include fish, swans, wedding bells or lovebirds. Ice cubes made from frozen punch won't water down anyone's drink. For a fancy look, freeze a piece of fruit — a strawberry, wedge of lemon, etc... — in each cube or float a mold of frozen punch (or wine, champagne) in the punch bowl.

Be creative and don't be afraid to suggest something different. Consider foods with a difference — quiche, beef stroganoff or dishes of Swedish meatballs. For a smaller group, tableside food preparation might prove interesting from the tossing of a Caesar salad to a chef preparing Chinese food in a wok to flambeed desserts. Including ethnic foods of your heritage is another option — potato pancakes, moussaka, stuffed grape leaves or pasta carbonara.

How about "monkey bread"? The name is as amusing and delightful as the eating of it. Quite simply, it is molded bread made from refrigerated biscuits and baked in a Turk's-head-shaped mold. The surprise comes when it's baked — it pulls apart into individual sections.

Fill old-fashioned candy jars with mints or almonds or create a warm glow with stately candles and glass swans filled with fresh fruit and flowers. Centerpieces highlight your whole tablesetting. How about ones you can eat? For example, baskets of sweet berries and cinnamon rolls or croissants or scrumptious varieties of cookies in decorated soft-sculpture or wicker baskets. Form table wreaths out of layers of cookies. Fill the center with flowers. How about decorated wedding boxes in the center of each table filled with caramel corn? How about pineapples (the symbol of hospitality) surrounded by mints and nuts? Fill baskets or decorative glass jars with Christmas candy, candy canes and cinnamon sticks, or perhaps chocolate truffles and strawberries serving as delicious finger desserts.

# — Notes to Myself —

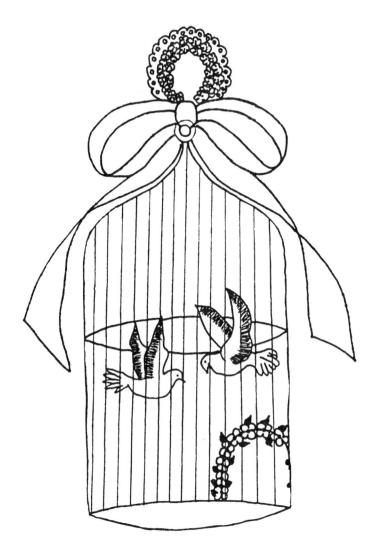

# Wedding Reception
## "Little Extras"

# WEDDING RECEPTION — LITTLE EXTRAS

1. Carry a wedding theme into your reception plans, ie: a valentine theme with Cupid, an oriental theme with hanging paper lanterns and pretty paper parasols (as drink mixers or favors), a country theme, an Hawaiian theme, a heritage theme, a fairy tale theme, rainbow theme, Holiday season, etc...

2. Substituting pale pink lightbulbs for the usual white ones can work wonders in giving your reception room a party atmosphere.

3. Consider a large felt banner saying "Just Married" or "We're Mr. & Mrs. Now".

4. Decorate your tables with little boxes brimming with almonds or other special favors.

5. Perhaps a pair of live doves (or other birds) in a decorated cage would add to the wedding atmosphere.

6. Place table vases or candles on each reception table. Design centerpieces around a spray of multi-colored candles. Use hand-dipped candles or set out squat candles to cast a cheery glow.

7. Consider specially decorated placecards at the head table; tiny easels with calligraphed names on posterboard squares.

8. For a burst of color, criss-cross solid color tablecloths with bright ribbon streamers.

9. Arrange flatware and napkins in packets for each guest. tuck them in tiny colored paper bags or secure the packets with hand-made napkin rings — perhaps fashioned as miniature garters or aprons.

10. Add distinction with an unusual napkin fold. Tuck fruit inside for an extra treat.

11. Tinkle a dinner bell as the "signal" that you are about to begin eating.

12.Children at the reception? Seat them with their parents, but after they have finished eating, have a game table set up in a corner of the room.

13.Step out on the dance floor with your maids and ushers.

14.Honor your parents in a special way by having the band play a special song for them; along with your song.

15.Request a special type of dance — ie, a square dance, polka or the hokey-pokey, etc....

16.Mingling with your guests is an important part of the reception. Why not circulate with your groom and a full platter of homemade cookies or candies?

17.Ask your caterer to pack you a box lunch. This way, no matter what time you reach your hotel, you'll have your own "picnic for two".

18.Share a day filled with fun! Stay until reception's end. After all, this is the most memorable party you will ever plan and attend.

Accessory Ideas

# ACCESSORY IDEAS

## Rice

Why not supply the rice for your guests? Cut nylon netting into circles measuring six inches in diameter. Use lace trim around the edge if desired. Fill with rice, gather edges and tie with a scented bow. Add posies, forget-me-nots or any other decorations. Your rice doesn't have to be put into traditional netting circles. Be original. Imagine crepe paper or silk tulips filled with rice to be thrown at you and your groom. Assign a special helper to pass out the rice tulips. Each guest retains a wedding day memento — the flower.

Why not dye the rice to match your wedding colors or make it multi-colored? Here's a recipe from the Rice Council: Mix 1 cup water with ½ to 1 teaspoon of food coloring (depending upon how much color you want) in a 1-quart glass or metal bowl. Add 2½ cups of uncooked rice and let stand for five minutes. Drain, reserving colored water for the next batch. Spread rice in the bottom of a baking pan and place in a pre-heated 250 degree oven for 15 minutes, stirring occasionally. Remove and let dry on paper towels. This makes enough to fill about 36 packets.

Instead of rice, try confetti or soft rose petals. Birdseed is also an alternative — a wise one — as you need not worry about clean-up.

## Ring Pillow

Personalize your ring pillow by adding something special to it, or make your own from velvet, satin or lace. It doesn't have to be round in shape. Consider a special form: wreath, swan, bell; pineapple, heart, lamb, doll, etc... or a special design. Embroider on it — perhaps "To Love and Cherish", or your initials and wedding date. A circle of pearls and tiny satin bows filled with flowers, a furry rabbit's foot or a horseshoe charm might decorate the center. Use velvet ribbon or braided satin to attach rings. If you're very cautious, you might choose to attach the real rings. The best man can remove them as the ring bearer reaches the end of the aisle during the processional.

## Ideas For Car Decorating...

...might include traditional use of tin cans and old shoes as well as streamers of crepe paper, felt hearts, balloons, bells, big white bows, flowers, pin-wheels and your own handmade bumper sticker designs.

## Favors

Give wedding favors that guests can keep as a memento or hang on their Christmas tree for years to come. Consider plastic baskets, miniature champagne glasses, swans or bells filled with white almond candies, colored mints and nuts or chocolate *Hershey's Kisses.*

Making favors offers a great opportunity to show your individuality — perhaps quilled snowflakes, small, handled-baskets fashioned from giftwrap or crocheted candy canes. Use miniature appliques, pipe cleaners, lace, candy hearts, ribbons, flowers, jingle bells, tiny picture frames, bud vases, rings, yarn, scrolls, powder puffs, tiny white plastic bells, feathers, velvet, satin, beads, sequins, sweet sachets, potpourri, etc....

Consider favor-like napkin rings of lace, ribbon and flowers or in the shape of miniature, decorated blue satin garters.

## More Accessory Ideas

Charms are cute mementos. An "I Caught the Bouquet" or "You're Next" charm inscribed with your names and wedding date will provide a long-lasting memory to the lucky maid. A similar token might be inscribed for the lucky bachelor. Consider "I Caught the Bouquet" and "I

Caught the Garter" signs to provide a unique wedding album photo.

Your element of luck might be a traditional sixpence, or perhaps, a tiny horseshoe or unicorn charm or even a four-leaf clover.

To mark those special pews reserved for family, consider candles, miniature Christmas trees, flower balls, hearts, swans, wedding bells or Cupids.

Use colorful balloons to brighten up your wedding day, especially at an outdoor wedding. Float them in every available nook — among the hedges, in the gazebo, tied to chairs and in the trees. Assign a special helper or have bridesmaids pass out balloons to guests after the ceremony. They might release them together as you and your groom come out the door. What a beautiful and original photograph this idea will make. Colorful foil and heart-shaped balloons are also available as well as balloons with wedding sayings like "Just Married" and "We're Mr. & Mrs. Now". Decorate your reception hall with balloon bouquets!

Sew a cover (from your dress fabric or your attendants' dress fabric) for your family Bible or the prayer book you might be carrying during the ceremony. If you're writing your own vows and want to be sure you will remember, have them printed on the inside cover.

An alternative to the traditional guest book? Why not design your own, complete with space for instant pictures with captions and your invitation imbedded in the cover. You might put "keepsake pockets" on the inside of the front and back covers. Something really unique? How about a brightly-colored tablecloth for holiday use during the years to come. Ask each guest to autograph the cloth as they enter the reception. Later, you might embroider the signatures.

Hang a festive wreath of welcome on the door to your home or the reception hall. Decorate with lace ribbons, silk flowers, bells, lovebirds, herbs, sachets, etc... This wreath could also be used for showers and at pre-nuptial parties.

Will you have a gift table at the reception complete with a decorated box for cards and gifts of money? Why not use a wishing well or a painted and decorated birdcage instead?

Visit a few craft bazaars prior to the wedding. With the boom in handmade crafts, many ideas could jump right out at you. For example, buy a lacy handkerchief and embroider it with a special message or purchase a fabric basket — add lace and flower petals for a unique flower girl's basket. You might even include whole flower stems and have your flower girl hand them to scattered guests on her way down the aisle.

A set of hand-painted ceramic or hand-sewn bride n' groom dolls will add charm as your head table center-piece. How about a ceramic cake platter printed with names and wedding date?

You might make your own special reception center-pieces or a bridal canopy for use at the reception hall entrance, just outside the church or over your cake and/or champagne fountain.

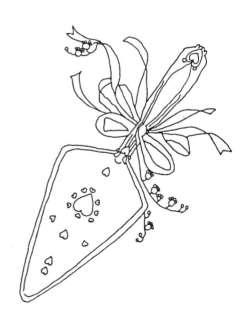

# After the Wedding

# AFTER THE WEDDING

The planning is finished and the "big day" is over. Here are a few "idea suggestions" for after the wedding:
1. Be creative when thanking your parents:
   a) Write a poem or special verse.
   b) Purchase wooden plaques with an engraved special message.
   c) Have a bouquet of balloons delivered the next day by a friend. Attach a gigantic thank you card with your special message.
   d) Call your parents when you reach your honeymoon destination and offer a special word of thanks.
   e) Send a telegram.
2. Preserve your wedding flowers.
3. Use your cakeknife. Don't pack it away. Simply change the color of the ribbon for special holiday use.
4. Instead of stuffing it away somewhere, frame and display your wedding certificate in your new home.
5. Ask your clergyman to bless your new home.
6. Make a Christmas tree ornament from your wedding favor.
7. Purchase and display a wedding photo frame with an area for your invitation as well as several pictures.
8. Preserve your wedding cards in a scrapbook. Cut each card down the fold, to place the front and inside messages side by side. Or, clip handwritten messages (with or without the verse) from your shower and wedding cards. Shape them into collages to fill scrapbook pages.
9. Decoupage or needlepoint a copy of your wedding invitation. Frame it in a soft-sculpture picture frame. Or, turn a wedding invitation into a treasured keepsake using the lovely old art of paper quilling.
10. Stuff a sweet sachet into your ring pillow. It can be a delightful addition to your bedroom.
11. If you used several candles in your wedding, melt them down to make one big candle that you can light each year at your anniversary. Glue or melt other wedding mementos onto the base of the candle such as lovebirds, cake decorations, silk flowers, ribbon, etc...
12. Monogram some of your wedding gifts such as silver, linens, etc...

# — Notes to Myself —

*In Closing....*

*... I would like to reiterate the importance of taking into consideration the feelings of family members and friends. Remember... it's the "little things" that may provide even more meaningful memories... a special remembrance for parents, a quiet moment with your younger sister just before the ceremony, something special for attendants, etc...*

*Other basic factors to be taken into consideration throughout your planning should include: family circumstances and lifestyles, local customs, dreams, season of the year and your overall budget.*

*Review this book as you progress through the decision-making process. For more ideas, review other wedding reference books and current bridal magazines.*

# — Notes to Myself —